The life we live is an encouragement itself. Document your Experiences, Testimonies and Success Stories as encouragement for your family or donate your book back to us. Your book will then be added to the Big Book of Encouragement Library as a reference for future generations.

IT'S BETTER TO BE
HOT OR COLD

WE CAN'T SERVE TWO MASTERS

WHEN DO YOU BELIEVE IT IS APPROPRIATE TO SWITCH FROM "SOFT" LOVE, WHICH EMPHASIZES SUPPORT AND COMPASSION, TO 'TOUGH' LOVE, WHICH USES MORE DIRECT METHODS OF DISCIPLINE?

It May Not Be an Easy Decision But

It's My Decision

TELL OF A TIME WHEN YOU HAD TO CHOOSE BETWEEN LISTENING TO THE POSITIVE VOICE AND NEGATIVE VOICE, WHICH DID YOU CHOOSE?

LET LOVE ARISE

Choices

WHAT EXPERIENCE OR CIRCUMSTANCE LED TO THE HARDENING OF YOUR HEART, AND WHAT HAVE YOU DONE OR WHAT HAS HAPPENED TO OPEN IT UP AGAIN?

Discipline is a cornerstone for personal growth

DISCIPLINE IS A CORNERSTONE OF PERSONAL GROWTH. IN WHAT WAYS HAVE YOU UTILIZED DISCIPLINE TO SHAPE YOUR VALUES, BELIEFS, AND CHARACTER?

_____

_____

_____

_____

_____

_____

_____

_____

_____

_____

_____

_____

_____

_____

_____

_____

_____

_____

_____

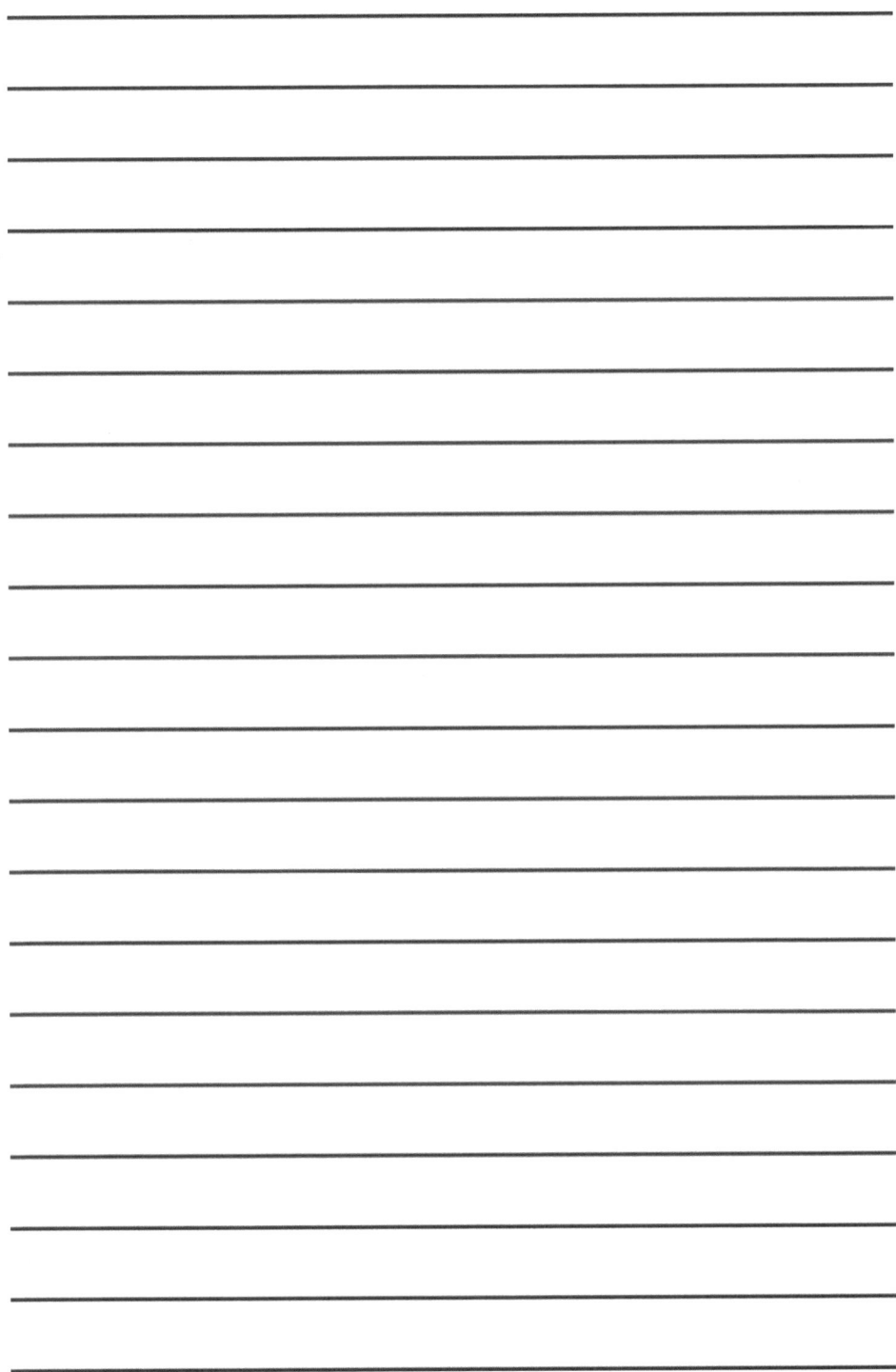

THE LIFE WE LIVE IS AN
ENCOURAGEMENT ITSELF.
THIS SECTION IS FOR REFLECTION, FOR
WE CANNOT FIX ANYONE OTHER THAN
OURSELVES.
TURNING OUR PROBLEMS INTO POWER.

Discipline: Each shot is Consistent and Controlled

NEXT TIME MY HEART IS ATTACKED I PRAY TO RECOGNIZE...

_____

_____

_____

_____

_____

_____

_____

_____

_____

_____

_____

_____

_____

_____

_____

_____

_____

_____

_____

_____

Another Day...
Another Chance to Try again!

IAmEncouragement

I PRAY TO BE SENSITIVE TO...

There's Always A Way Out

IamEncouragement

I PRAY FOR THE ABILITY TO ...

_____

_____

_____

_____

_____

_____

_____

_____

_____

_____

_____

_____

_____

_____

_____

_____

_____

_____

_____

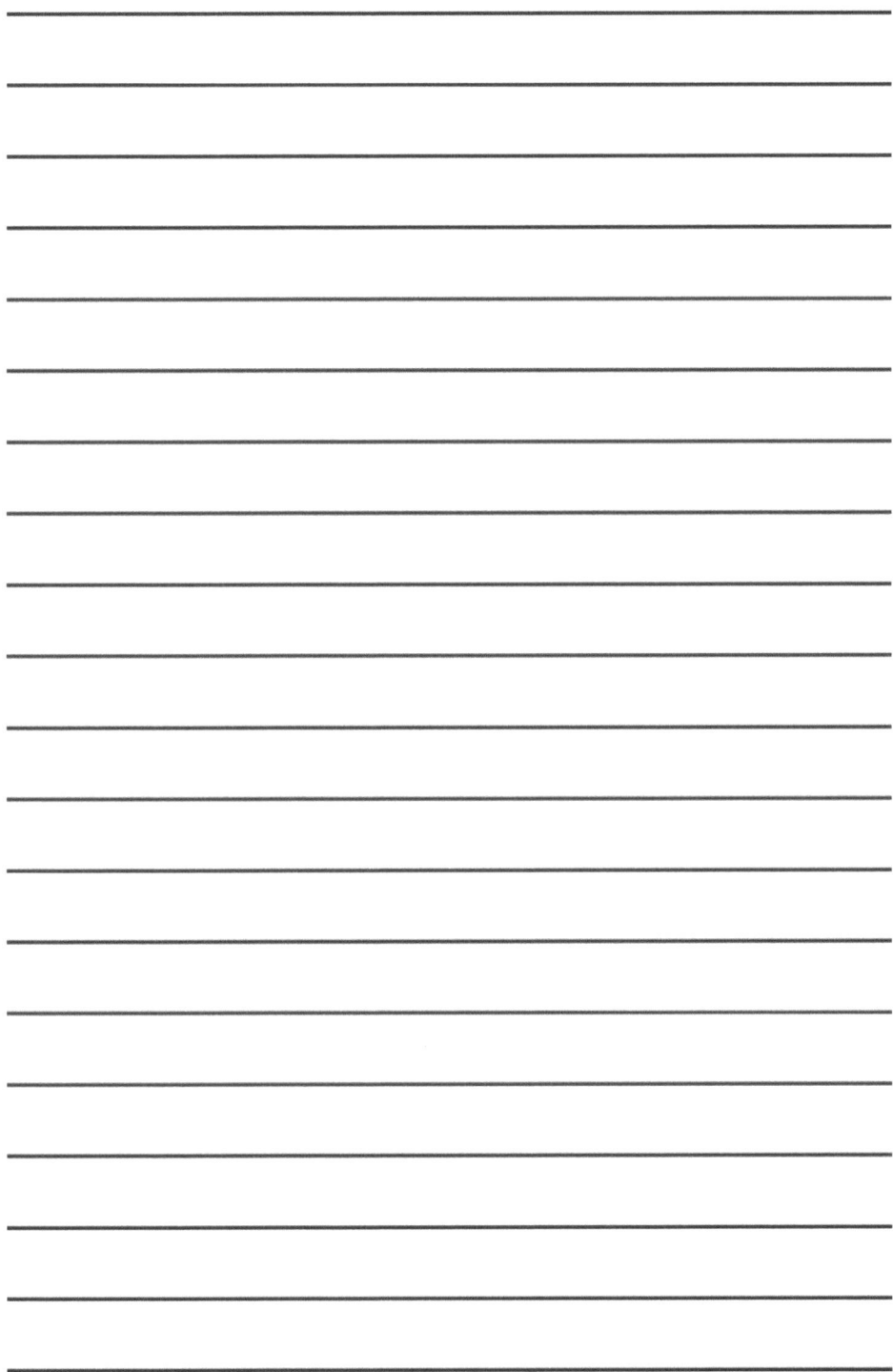

We have to make choices daily so this section is Free Writing. Discover the root of things by writing the:
Who, What, When, Why & How